A GI

D0720843

FROM:

DATE:

CRAZY ABOUT MISTLETOE™

COPYRIGHT © 2003 BY MARK GILROY COMMUNICATIONS, INC.
TULSA, OKLAHOMA

ART AND DESIGN BY JACKSONDESIGNCO,LLC
SILOAM SPRINGS, ARKANSAS

ISBN 1-59310-425-1

PUBLISHED BY BARBOUR PUBLISHING, INC., P.O. BOX 719,
UHRICHSVILLE, OHIO 44683, www.barbourpublishing.com

Member of the
Evangelical Christian
Publishers Association

PRINTED IN CHINA.

"GLORY TO GOD IN THE HIGHEST,
AND ON EARTH PEACE,
GOODWILL TOWARD MEN!"

LUKE 2:14

CONTENTS

Savor and Celebrate!

The holidays are here, and it truly is the most wonderful time of year. Visiting family and friends...giving and receiving gifts...beautiful music filling airwaves and joyfully singing favorite carols...children's pageants and television specials new and old...blazing neon lights and gently flickering candles...bell ringers collecting money for the poor...jostling crowds at the mall and a Christmas card from an old friend...the tempting aroma of cookies wafting through the house...reading a long-neglected book and attending one more party...boisterous family games and reflecting on the manger scene beautifully arranged on the mantel...

In the hustle and bustle of your incredibly active life, slow down, pause, stop...savor...celebrate the sights, sounds, stories, and meaning of the holidays!

I'M CRAZY ABOUT GIFTS
BECAUSE OF THE JOY OF SHOPPING.

I'M CRAZY ABOUT GIFTS
BECAUSE IT'S FUN SHAKING BOXES.

I'M CRAZY ABOUT GIFTS
BECAUSE THE BEST ONES
DON'T ALWAYS COST MONEY.

I'M CRAZY ABOUT GIFTS
BECAUSE THEY'RE AS GREAT
TO GIVE AS THEY ARE TO RECEIVE.

I'M CRAZY ABOUT GIFTS
BECAUSE GOD GAVE US THE
GREATEST GIFT OF ALL.

What Can I Give Him?

What can I give Him,
Poor as I am?
If I were a shepherd
I would bring a lamb.
If I were a wise man
I would do my part.
Yet what I can I give Him,
Give my heart.

CHRISTINA ROSSETTI

Gift-Giving Reminders

GIVE TO OTHERS ~ Remember those who don't have much
this time of year. Write a check to a group like
the Salvation Army. Buy gifts for needy children through
Toys for Tots, the Angel Tree program for children
of prisoners, or another worthy local organization.

GIVE TO THOSE YOU LOVE ~ Remember the best gifts don't necessarily cost the most money—give the gift of yourself and your time. Create "I love you" coupons that can be redeemed throughout the year. For example, a certificate to attend a baseball game or amusement park in the summer would be loved by your son or daughter.

GIVE TO THOSE WHO SERVE ~ Remember the people who have served you this year—hair stylists, mail deliverers, teachers, ministers—with a small token of appreciation.

GIVE WITHOUT GOING BROKE ~ Remember to be generous, but don't overspend and pay for Christmas all through next year!

Chestnuts roasting on an open fire...

I'M CRAZY ABOUT HOLIDAY MUSIC
BECAUSE IT MAKES MY PARENTS GET
ALL MUSHY.

I'M CRAZY ABOUT HOLIDAY MUSIC
BECAUSE OUR NEIGHBORHOOD
IS LOADED WITH TALENT.

And as long as you love me so,
let it snow, let it snow, let it snow!

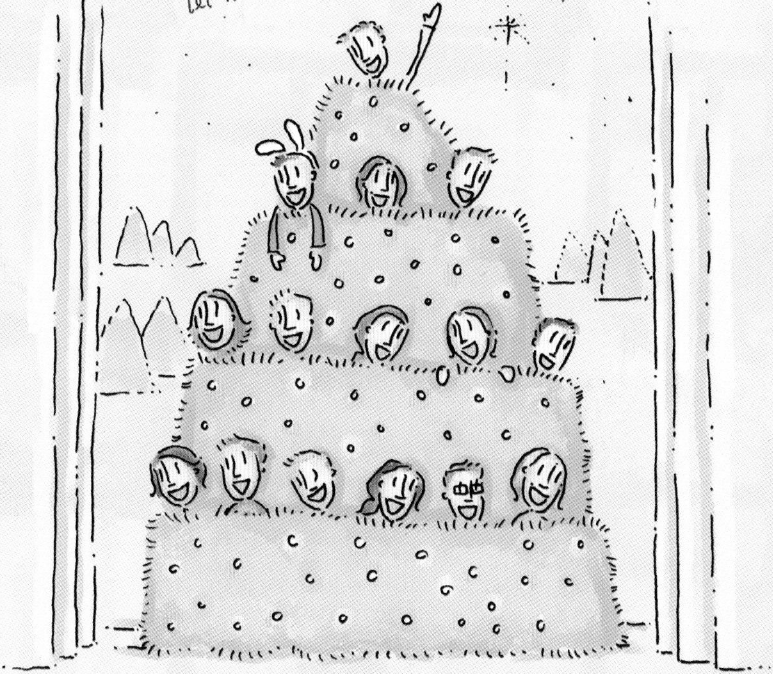

I'M CRAZY ABOUT HOLIDAY MUSIC
BECAUSE OF THE PAGEANTS AT SCHOOL.

I'M CRAZY ABOUT HOLIDAY MUSIC
BECAUSE IT INSPIRES ANNUAL
TELEVISION SPECIALS THAT ARE PERFECT
FOR THE WHOLE FAMILY.

Silent Night... Holy Night...

I'M CRAZY ABOUT HOLIDAY MUSIC
BECAUSE IT WARMS MY HEART.

♪

Silent Night

The organ of a small church in Arndorf, Austria, had fallen into disrepair. The parish priest, Father Josef Mohr, was troubled that his poor congregation had no money for repairs—and the Christmas season was at hand.

On the day before Christmas Eve, as he trudged home from visiting a family that had lost a loved one, he was awestruck by the beauty of the surrounding mountains and his peaceful village in the valley below. When he arrived home, he quickly penned the words to a poem inspired by the moment.

He read his poem to a musician, Franz Gruber, the next day. Gruber was so captivated by the words that he wrote a melody to be played on his guitar.

"Silent Night" premiered on Christmas morning in 1818 and has been sung by millions in the centuries that have followed.

I Heard the Bells on Christmas Day

WRITTEN BY HENRY WADSWORTH LONGFELLOW IN 1863,
DURING THE DARKEST HOURS OF THE CIVIL WAR.

I heard the bells on Christmas Day
Their old familiar carols play,
And wild and sweet the words repeat
Of peace on earth, good will to men.

I thought how, as the day had come,
The belfries of all Christendom
Had rolled along the unbroken song
of peace on earth, good will to men.

And in despair I bowed my head.
"There is no peace on earth," I said,
"For hate is strong, and mocks the song
Of peace on earth, good will to men."

Then pealed the bells more loud and deep:
"God is not dead, nor doth He sleep;
The wrong shall fail, the right prevail
With peace on earth, good will to men."

Till ringing, singing on its way,
They were revolved from night to day—
A voice, a chime, chant sublime,
Of peace on earth good will to men.

I'M CRAZY ABOUT COOKIES AND TREATS
BECAUSE THEY HAVE NO CALORIES
THIS TIME OF YEAR.

Grandma's Cookie Cutter Sugar Cookies

RECIPE

Have a decorating party with lots of colors of icing and sprinkles!

Cream together: **1/2 C. MARGARINE, 3/4 C. SUGAR**

Beat in: **1 EGG , 1 1/2 TSP. VANILLA**. Sift together: **1 1/2 C. FLOUR,**

1 TSP. BAKING POWDER, 1/4 TSP. SALT

Mix together and chill in refrigerator for eight hours.

Roll on a floured surface; cut with cookie cutter shapes.

Bake 8–10 minutes at 350° or until edges barely brown.

ICING:

Mix: **2½ C. CONFECTIONERS' SUGAR, 4 TBSP. MELTED BUTTER**

Beat in: **1 EGG WHITE**. Add: **2–3 TBSP. CREAM**

and more **SUGAR** until good spreading consistency.

Kids love decorating!

The Fudgiest Fudge

RECIPE

18 OZ. PACKAGE SEMISWEET CHOCOLATE CHIPS

1 CAN SWEETENED CONDENSED MILK

DASH OF SALT

1½ TSP. VANILLA

½ TSP. ALMOND EXTRACT

½ C. BLACK WALNUTS (OPTIONAL)

Melt chocolate chips and condensed milk
in microwave for one minute.

Stir and then put in microwave for another minute.
Add salt, vanilla, almond extract,
and walnuts. Stir thoroughly.

Pour mixture onto waxed paper lined pan.
Cool for two hours in refrigerator.

Turn onto a board and cut into pieces.

Rosy Mulled Cider

RECIPE

2 QT. APPLE JUICE

1 C. ORANGE JUICE

¼ C. CINNAMON CANDIES

12 WHOLE CLOVES

Combine all ingredients and bring to a boil.
Strain out cloves and serve hot
with orange slice for garnishing.

Warm and spicy!

A Gift from Your Kitchen!

Hot Spiced Tea

RECIPE

1/2 C. INSTANT LEMON TEA

2 C. POWDERED ORANGE DRINK

1 TSP. CINNAMON

1 TSP. GROUND CLOVES

2 1/2 C. SUGAR

Mix all ingredients thoroughly and store in a tin,
glass jar, or other decorative container. Tie with
a ribbon and send home with guests who stop
by your home during the holidays.

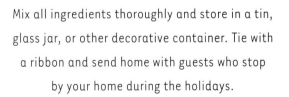

English Toffee Bars

RECIPE

30 "CLUB" CRACKERS   1 C. BROWN SUGAR

1 C. BUTTER   12 OZ. CHOCOLATE CHIPS

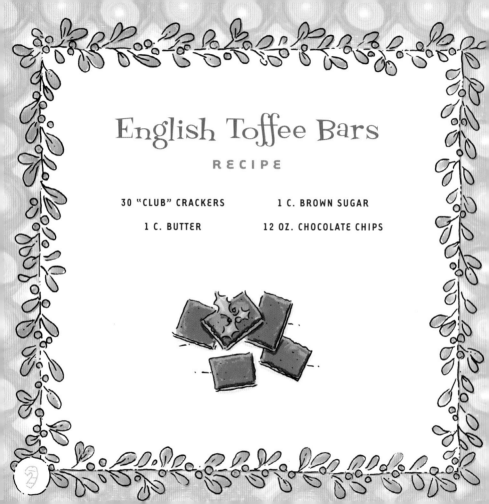

Heavily grease a 9" x 13" baking pan.

Arrange crackers over the pan.

In a saucepan, combine sugar and butter.

Bring to a boil for four minutes while stirring constantly.

Pour over crackers and place in 400° oven
for eight minutes or until bubbly.

Sprinkle with chocolate chips.
Use spatula to evenly spread melted chocolate
over the bubbly mixture.

Chill at least two hours in refrigerator,
then break or cut into pieces.

Christmas
Wreath Cookies

RECIPE

Use a cookie press to make these pretty green cookies that everybody loves!

Cream together:

½ C. BUTTER   **1½ OZ. CREAM CHEESE**

¼ C. SUGAR   **½ TSP. VANILLA**

Sift in:

1 C. FLOUR

Add green food coloring. Chill one hour. Put in a cookie press
and use the star-shaped form. Make into small circles
on cookie sheet. Add cinnamon candy dots for holly berries.

Bake at 400° for 8–10 minutes or until edges barely brown.

Yields 2 dozen.

Gingerbread Men

RECIPE

1/3 C. SHORTENING

1 C. LIGHT BROWN SUGAR, PACKED

1 1/2 C. LIGHT MOLASSES

6 C. ALL-PURPOSE FLOUR

2 TSP. BAKING SODA

1/2 TSP. SALT

1 TSP. ALLSPICE

1 TSP. GINGER

1 TSP. CLOVES

1 TSP. CINNAMON

Mix first three ingredients together, and then sift
in remaining dry ingredients. Chill in refrigerator overnight.

Roll dough ¼-inch thick. Cut cookies
with gingerbread man form.

Place on lightly greased cookie sheet
and bake at 350° for 15 minutes. Yields 4 dozen.

I'M CRAZY ABOUT MISTLETOE
AND OUR ENTHUSIASTIC NEIGHBORS.

I'M CRAZY ABOUT MISTLETOE
AND FAMILY TRADITIONS.

I'M CRAZY ABOUT MISTLETOE
AND A FIRE IN THE FIREPLACE.

I'M CRAZY ABOUT MISTLETOE
AND HANDMADE ORNAMENTS.

I'M CRAZY ABOUT MISTLETOE
BECAUSE ROMANCE IS IN THE AIR.

For the Birds!

Help take care of the winter birds in your area.
When you take down your Christmas tree, set it
up in your backyard as a "feed the birds" tree.

Decorate with long strands of popcorn and dry cereal.
Add pinecones that have been covered in
peanut butter and rolled in bird seed.

Hang on to Those Memories

One of the most popular hobbies today is
creating an elaborate family "scrapbook"
with highly stylized pages for each year.

Maybe such a task seems too daunting to undertake.
Or perhaps you are already a veteran of
"creative memories," including Christmas pages.

Either way, consider starting a memory notebook that
puts all your Christmas memories in one notebook.

Should you start with this year or include previous years?
Go back as many years as you have pictures for, of course!

As you work on current years, supplement family pictures
with memorable Christmas cards received, programs
from church services and other special moments,
and pictures of current events to remind family members
what was happening in the world that year.

Make sure you place in a prominent place
each year so family and friends can enjoy!

I'M CRAZY ABOUT FAMILY
BECAUSE OF FRIENDLY AND
"SPIRITED" GAME NIGHTS.

I'M CRAZY ABOUT FRIENDS
BECAUSE THEY LOVE ME AS I AM.

(AND HELP ME WHEN I'M DESPERATE!)

Could you use some help getting
ready for your in-laws coming to town?

I'M CRAZY ABOUT FAMILY
BECAUSE WHEN WE GATHER
AT GRANDMA'S HOUSE WE FEEL
SO CLOSE TO EACH OTHER.

I'M CRAZY ABOUT FRIENDS
BECAUSE THEY GIVE
SUCH THOUGHTFUL GIFTS.

Oh, wow...you shouldn't have... cause, like, uh, yours won't be in until tomorrow, uh...

I'M CRAZY ABOUT FAMILY
BECAUSE NO MATTER HOW
FAR AWAY YOU MIGHT GO,
YOU CAN ALWAYS COME HOME.

I'M CRAZY ABOUT FRIENDS
BECAUSE THEY FORGIVE AND FORGET.

6 Family Activity Ideas

THESE IDEAS WORK GREAT FOR A GROUP OF GOOD FRIENDS AS WELL!

MIXED GAME NIGHT ~ Combine shortened versions of Pictionary, Trivial Pursuit, Cranium, Monopoly, and other family favorites.

HOLIDAY CLASSIC ~ Select a wholesome family movie like *It's a Wonderful Life*, *White Christmas*, *The Fourth Wise Man*, or *Miracle on 34th Street* to watch together.

LIGHTS OF THE CITY ~ Load up in the car and drive through neighborhoods and business areas that have great Christmas displays. Stop by a church that is hosting an outdoor "living nativity" scene.

GREAT NEIGHBORS ~ Work together to wrap up homemade treats or other small gifts to take to the neighbors. Have the whole family deliver them.

HELPING HANDS ~ Volunteer as a family to help out in a soup kitchen or other outreach program for the needy. Discuss the joy of giving—not just receiving—during the holiday season.

THE CHRISTMAS STORY ~ On Christmas Eve or Christmas morning, gather as a family to read Luke 2, the most complete biblical account of the Christmas story. Or select a classic from literature, such as Henry Van Dyke's *The Other Wise Man*.

THE MOST IMPORTANT ACTIVITY OF ALL IS
SIMPLY SPENDING TIME WITH THOSE YOU LOVE!

Welcome to My Home

• the sweet aroma of spicy candles and potpourri

• homemade baked goodies ready to serve

• a CD player loaded with the Christmas music
of Nat King Cole, Percy Faith, Kenny G, and
other classic and contemporary artists

• candles, candles, candles everywhere—to add sparkle on tables, countertops, bathroom shelves, and anywhere else that is safe

• a fire—real or otherwise—in the fireplace

• a small, inexpensive gift to warm the heart of all who enter your home—like a book!

Coming Home

And I do come home at Christmas.

We all do, or we all should.

We all come home,

or ought to come home,

for a short holiday—

the longer, the better.

CHARLES DICKENS

I'M CRAZY ABOUT HOLIDAY STORIES
BECAUSE KIDS OF ALL AGES
STILL LOVE THE GRINCH.

"And it came to pass in those days that a decree went out from Caesar Augustus..."

I'M CRAZY ABOUT HOLIDAY VERSE BECAUSE IT BONDS FAMILIES TOGETHER.

The Legend of St. Nicholas

Saint Nick. Father Christmas. Bonhomme Noel.
Knecht Clobes. Who is the real Santa Claus?

In the fourth century, a young man named
Nicholas was left a small fortune upon the
death of his parents. He quickly gave away
all his wealth to charity, particularly
in ways that benefited children.

With his money gone, he became a monk. Though content
to live in obscurity, his legend continued to grow,
and he was appointed as the Bishop of Myra, Lucia.

Nicholas was eventually adopted as the
patron saint of Russia. His day is celebrated in
that country on December 6 of each year.

The exchanging of gifts, practiced in different
ways around the world, is not only based
on the gifts of the magi, but also the legend
of Nicholas's benevolence toward children.

Long, Long Ago

Winds through the olive trees
Softly did blow,
'Round little Bethlehem
Long, long ago.

Sheep on the hillside lay
Whiter than snow.
Shepherds were watching them,
Long, long ago.

Then from the happy sky,
Angels bent low,
Singing their song of joy,
Long, long ago.

For in a manger bed,
Cradled we know,
Christ came to Bethlehem,
Long, long ago.

ANONYMOUS

Yes, Virginia, There Is a Santa Claus

NOT EVERYONE AGREES ON HOW MUCH CREDENCE OR EMPHASIS SHOULD BE GIVEN TO SANTA CLAUS WHEN IT COMES TO CHILDREN. BUT AN EDITOR FOR *THE NEW YORK SUN,* ON SEPTEMBER 21, 1897, CERTAINLY CAPTURED THE ESSENCE OF FAITH IN RESPONSE TO THE FOLLOWING LETTER:

Dear Editor,

I am eight years old. Some of my little friends say there is no Santa Claus. Papa says, "If you see it in the *Sun* it's so." Please tell me the truth, is there a Santa Claus?

VIRGINIA O'HANLON
115 WEST 95TH STREET

Virginia, your little friends are wrong. They have been affected by the skepticism of a skeptical age. They do not believe except they see. They think that nothing can be which is not comprehensible by their little minds.

Yes, Virginia, there is a Santa Claus. He exists as certainly as love and generosity and devotion exist, and you know that they abound and give to your life its highest beauty and joy. Alas! How dreary would be the world if there were no Santa Claus! It would be as dreary as if there were no Virginias. There would be no childlike faith then, no poetry, no romance to make tolerable this existence. We should have no enjoyment, except in sense and sight. The eternal light with which childhood fills the world would be extinguished.

Not believe in Santa Claus! The most real things in the world are those that neither children nor men can see.

Excerpted

He Knew How
to Keep Christmas

Scrooge was better than his word. He did all
and infinitely more; and to Tiny Tim he became
a second father. He became as good a friend,
as good a master, and as good a man as the good
old city knew, or any other good old city,
town, or borough in the good old world.
Some people laughed to see the alteration in him;
but his own heart laughed,
and that was quite enough for him.

It was always said of him, that he knew how to keep
Christmas well if any man alive possessed the knowledge.

May that be truly said of us, and all of us!

And so, as Tiny Tim observed, "God Bless Us, Every One!"

ABRIDGED FROM *A CHRISTMAS CAROL*

BY CHARLES DICKENS

A Christmas Prayer

Loving Father, help us remember the birth
of Jesus, that we may share in the song
of the angels, the gladness of the shepherds,
and the worship of the wise men.

Close the door of hate and open
the door of love all over the world.

Let kindness come with every gift
and good desires with every greeting.

Deliver us from evil by the blessing which Christ brings,
and teach us to be merry with clear hearts.

May the Christmas morning make us happy to be
Thy children, and the Christmas evening bring us to
our beds with grateful thoughts, forgiving
and forgiven, for Jesus' sake. Amen!

ROBERT LOUIS STEVENSON

ALSO AVAILABLE:

CRAZY ABOUT MY CAT

CRAZY ABOUT MY DAUGHTER

CRAZY ABOUT MY DOG

CRAZY ABOUT MY FRIEND

CRAZY ABOUT MY GRANDPARENTS

CRAZY ABOUT MY SISTER

CRAZY ABOUT MY MOM

CRAZY ABOUT MY DAD

CRAZY ABOUT MY HUSBAND

CRAZY ABOUT MY WIFE

CRAZY ABOUT CHRISTMAS

CRAZY ABOUT YOU

CRAZY ABOUT MY TEACHER

CRAZY ABOUT CHOCOLATE